CADILLAC

CADILLAC

David Fetherston

Acknowledgements

Cadillacs have always been my favourite American car. From my earliest recollections as a 'car crazy' ten-year-old who spent hours madly scanning every *Saturday Evening Post, National Geographic, Life* and *Look* for automobile ads, it is the Cadillac advertisements that I remember the most. They represented a luxury world that was only found in America. In Australia their detractors called them Yank Tanks, Bloomingdales Barges and Road Whales. But none of that counted a scrap: driving a Cadillac was a nirvana that no foreign car, bar a Ferrari, could even hope to give its owner. I knew that when I was ten years old. I had read the ads. I would like to thank the owners of the Cadillacs we photographed for their time and interest. Special thanks to Ed Pashukewich in Livonia, Michigan for making Detroit 'happen', Wray Tibbs in Sacramento and to Don Frolich. I would also like to thank Mike Chase for his able assistance with the photography; Nanette Simmons for her assistance and persistence; Cori Ewing for his help with captions and photography. I also need to thank the great folks at Cadillac Public Relations: Bill O'Neil, Chuck Harrington, Ann Marie Sylvester and Al Haas, curator of the Cadillac Historic Collection, and without whose help I would never have completed this project.

Most of the photographs in this book were taken with a Mamiya RB 6X7 Pros S camera system. It's a great machine. Just like a Cadillac. The film stock was Fuji RDP 100, superbly processed by The Lab in Santa Rosa, California. Other photos came from Cadillac historic or GM Photographic sources. Extra-special thanks to Gloria for all her steadfastness and editorial help in bringing *CADILLAC* to completion.

Dedication
For Kate, my car-lovin' friend

Published in 1993 by Osprey, an imprint of Reed Consumer Books, Michelin House, 81 Fulham Road, London SW3 6RB and Auckland, Melbourne, Singapore and Toronto

© Reed International Books 1993

ISBN 185532 328 1

Editor Shaun Barrington
Page design Paul Kime
Printed in Hong Kong

Front cover
1959 Cadillac Convertible owned by Rudy and Mazz Vandenberg. Photographed at the Australian Institute of Science, Canberra (Photo Peter Bateman Street Machine Australia)

Right
Reproduced here with the permission of publishers' Kitchen Sink Press of Princeton, Wisconsin, Cadillacs and Dinosaurs is a wonderful book by Mark Schultz. Filled with adventure cartoons 'where time is out of kilter' according to its author and illustrator, this book is a

For a catalogue of all books published by Osprey Automotive please write to:

The Marketing Department, Reed Consumer Books, 1st Floor, Michelin House, 81 Fulham Road, London SW3 6RB

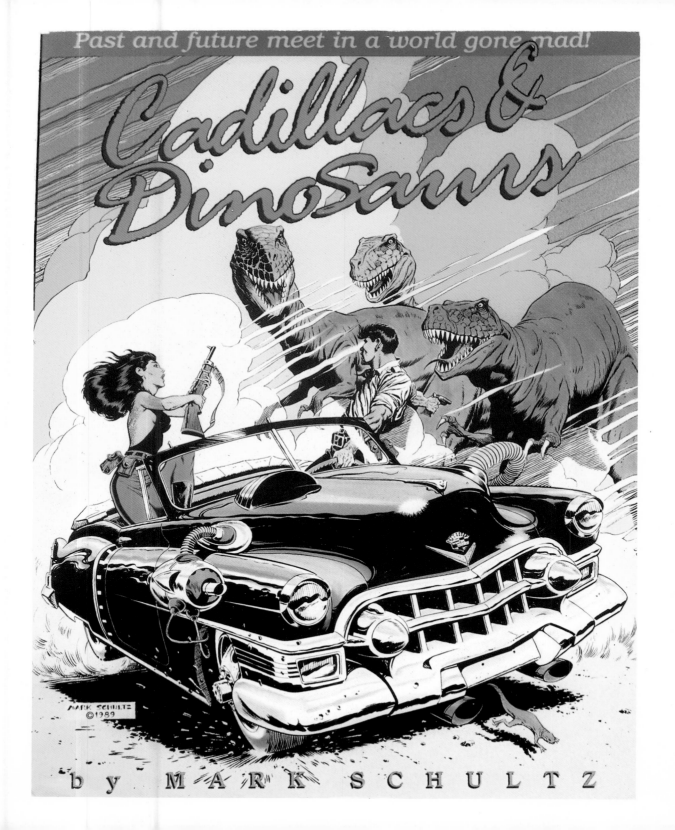

Common V8 Models '46 to '93

Year	Engine size	Horsepower	Models
1946	346	150	5
1947	346	150	11
1948	346	150	10
1949	331	160	13
1950/51	331	160	10
1952	331	190	7
1953	331	210	8
1954	331	230	8
1955	331	250/270	8
1956	365	285/305	10
1957	365	300/325	13
1958	365	310/325	13
1959/60	390	325/345	14
1961	390	325	12
1962	390	325	13
1963	390	325	12
1964/65	429	340	11
1966/67	429	340	12
1968/69	472	375	11
1970	472/500(E)	373/400	11
1971/72	472/500(E)	373/400	9
1973	472/500(E)	220/220/235	9
1974	472/500(E)	220/205/210	9
1975	350/500(E)	180/190	10
1976	350/500(E)	180/190	9
1977	350/425(E)	180/180	7
1978	350/425(E)	170/180	7
1979	350/425(E)	170/180	8
1980	250/350/368	124/105/150	8
1981	250/350/368	124/105/150	9
1982	250/350/368	105/125/150	9
1983	250/350/368	105/105/150	9
1984	250/350/368	105/125/150	9
1985	4.1/5.0	105/125	12
1986	4.1/5.0	130/140	10
1987	4.1/5.0	130/140	9
1988	4.5/5.0	155/140	8
1989	4.5/4.5/5.0	155/200/140	10
1990	4.5/5.0/5.7	180/140/175	10
1991	4.9/5.0/5.7	200/170/185	8
1992	4.9/5.0/5.7	200/170/185	11
1993	4.9/4.6/5.7	200/295/185	7

E = Eldorado

Contents

Introduction

During World War 2, Cadillac's industrial muscle was used to build tanks and aero engines, and the overriding priority of this task meant that there was little time to design new automobiles and tool-up for post-war production. The result was that the '46 and '47 Cadillacs looked little different from their pre-war brothers and sisters. With Harley Earl in the designer's seat, Cadillac took off with aircraft styling, fins and all. The great American post-war car boom was upon them and Earl's slick design work showed the way with new styles. He brought the fenders inside the bodyline and added sedanet bodies and cute fins. Cadillac could not produce enough cars and tens of thousands of orders went unfilled.

The 1950s also brought new and exciting cars the public wanted to see. Wonder cars such as the Cadillac Cyclone gave the public a taste of what the future could bring. Cadillacs were now growing in size and performance and could be optioned with engines producing over 300 horsepower. The fifties were brought to a close with the biggest fins of all on the '59 models.

The beginning of the sixties at Cadillac saw a dramatic reduction in the size of the fins and improvements in build quality and performance. The first front-wheel drive Cadillac arrived as the '67 Eldorado. A V12 had been designed and tested but a 429 cubic inch V8 was finally selected. The new Eldorado was designed by Bill Mitchell. This stunning new Eldorado coupe would spawn a generation of models that stretched into the end of the 1980s.

The 'oil wars' of the seventies would force Cadillac to 'down-size' its model line-up. This energy crunch which wanted high gas mileage econo-cars immediately had a battering effect on Cadillac and it took years to recover its gloss and gleam as America's premier luxury automobile manufacturer.

The 1980s showed just how resilient American manufacturers can be. Cadillac turned the ball game around by working on new and innovative products and production methods. The whole model line, less the Brougham, became front-wheel drive and over the decade the quality and style that Cadillac had represented earlier this century started to return. The nineties are Cadillac's decade of promise and judging by the fabulous new Seville and Eldorado that have just arrived on the scene, what is to come before the end of the decade should once again place Cadillac on the mark as 'The Standard of the World'.

The Cadillac Historic Collection in Detroit is only open to special interest tour groups but has many of Cadillac's greatest automobiles on display

Above
The Cadillac Cyclone was a hit on the auto show circuit in the early 1950s. Its space age styling put it light years ahead of anything else on wheels

Right
The experimental V12 that was tested for use in the '67 Eldorado. But it would be the 429 V8 which would win the day in the end. Bill Mitchell's design for the 1967 Eldorado coupe would prove to be a stylistic influence for the next two decades

The Cimarron Dual Cowl Phaeton was built as a show car and as a Pace Car for PPG CART racing. This fully functional concept car now resides in the Cadillac Historic Collection

Cadillac 1945 to 1950

The end of World War 2 did not automatically bring about the return of civilian automobile production, which had been stopped in 1941. It took time to re-establish production lines. Cadillac's assembly plants had spent the war making tanks and aircraft engines. The engineering staff had also been switched to war related design and engineering. Materials for civilian consumer products were scarce immediately after the conflict and the manufacturers who did get back into production soon found that what they wanted to build and what they could build added up to two different products. But this was not the biggest problem. During the war years very little had been done to design products for post-war production; the first vehicles off the assembly lines in late 1945-46 were simply '42 models to get the production lines going again.

The demand for new cars was staggering. In 1947 Cadillac had 200,000 vehicle orders but failed to fill 96,000 of them that year. However, 1948 was another story. Harley Earl became the 'King of Fin' when he introduced a new line of Cadillacs complete with eye-catching tailfins; these were thought to be inspired by the twin-boom Lockheed P-38 long-range fighter. The only model without fins in 1948 was the Series 75. The most gracious and memorable of these new styles was the Club Coupe sedanet fastback. This new post-war look featured a flattened hood and moulded fenders that fitted flush with the bodylines. The result of a collaborative effort by Earl and his assistants and associates Julio Andrade, Bill Mitchell, Frank Hershey and Art Ross, the 'new look' included built-in bumpers, clean and smooth bodywork and 24 psi low pressure tyres. Earl's only problem was that his new design was still powered by virtually the same flathead pre-war V8.

The big news for 1949 was the new overhead valve V8. It also signalled the delivery of the one millionth Cadillac, which was sold on 25 November 1949. The engine was the first of the great General Motors OHV V8s. Sized at 331 cubic inches, it developed 160 gross horsepower and weighed 200 pounds less than the old flathead. Engine development was overseen by John F Gordon and later Harry F Barr and Edward N Cole. This project proved to be the making of Ed Cole and he went to become one of world's foremost engine designers. In 1955 Cole introduced the most successful V8 of all time, the 265 cubic inch small block Chevrolet V8. This engine flowered into the LT1 in the current Corvette.

The Sixty One coupe has a fender design that was retired in '42 on all but the Seventy Five in favour of the fade-away design. Although technically the second to last of the pre-war Cadillacs, the '41 was the last exclusively pre-war design as the '42 was carried over into '46. The '42 line also saw the last of the side engine vents which were down to one per side from the previous years' multiple versions

The end of the decade also heralded some other notable achievements. Briggs Cunningham took his Cadillacs to tenth and eleventh overall in the French Le Mans 24 Hour road race. A new standard hydramatic transmission became available. The Sixty-One was beginning to be phased out while the 'Debutante Convertible' showcar, featuring leopard skin interior, gold plated interior trim and dissolved fish scales in the paint to give it a pearlescent sheen, dazzled a car-hungry public. The century had turned its first 50 years and Cadillac headlined their advertising with the call 'Distinguished Beyond All Others'. Buyers were still clammering for new cars and Cadillac were working on building the best that American wanted.

Above
After the war, materials and new designs were scarce. Cadillac production was aided by the fact that they brought in more money per pound of steel than any other GM division, thus they were given more material than the other divisions. Even with GM favouring Cadillac and the lack of an original design, almost fifty per cent of the orders could not be met. The '46 Sixty Two sedanet design differed from the '42 only in detail, such as the small rectangular grille-lights instead of the round ones in the pre-war design (Owner: Vince Gregoire)

Left
The new grille styling for '41 was broader and lower from the previous year. The wider grille was part of a trend that would take Cadillacs from tall and long to low, wide, and long. The exquisite grillework also shows the start of a trend from a mesh-like fine grille, to a separate bar-type grille. This style of grille work would remain a Cadillac feature until 1948

Above

The new five horizontal bar grille of the '47 no longer has the grille lights of the previous models. Behind the grille is also the same flathead engine as in 1946. With a 7.25 to 1 compression ratio this 346 cubic inch L-head produced 150 hp

Right

The '47 Cadillacs were virtually the same as the '42 or '46, but received some revisions and detail changes. This Series Sixty One five-passenger sedan uses the same five-bar grille as the Sixty and Sixty Two. This Series Sixty One is fitted with a Hydramatic transmission, white sidewalls, a radio, and an underseat heater. The sunvisor is an old aftermarket option This sporty Series Sixty One features the GM 'B-body' fastback styling which was used by all GM divisions for some models. Harley Earl picked up on this concept and used it very successfully with the late forties Cadillac sedanet (Owner: Ray Savage)

Above

The Series Seventy Five continued the '41 styling until the 1950 model year when the 'limos' were restyled with the other Cadillacs. Trim and grille changes were made in the intervening years, with some styling changes coming only a year after those of the smaller lines. This horizontal five bar grille belongs to a '48 model (Owner: David France)

Right

In lieu of a complete restyling, detail changes were made and the trim was modernised. As seen on this '48 Series Seventy Five, the post-war limos no longer had the side engine bay vents. Horizontal slashes were gone from the trailing edge of the front and rear fenders but true running-boards remained. Chrome trim on the lower edge of the rear fenders continued these running boards to the rear of the front fenders

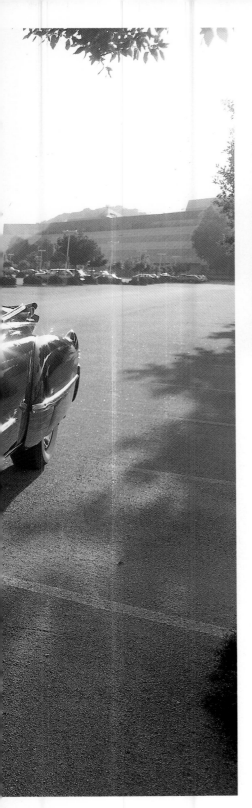

Above

The complete change of style carried on into the interior in 1948 with a pleasing new dash panel featuring a huge analog speedo using small secondary instruments along the base of the dash. A 16-inch steering wheel capped with a matching huge horn ring 'wheeled' the car about. The '48 came with low pressure tyres designed to run at 24 psi; this made the steering considerably heavier at lower speeds and ultimately led to Cadillac incorporating power steering as a standard feature in later years

Left

It took nearly four years for Cadillac to get its first true post-war model into the dealers' showrooms. This fine '48 Series Sixty Two convertible shows how gracefully Harley Earl and his assistant Julio Andrade worked to create the 'new look' for Cadillac, tailfins and all. His Lockheed P-38 inspired tailfins took the public by surprise as did the gracious, fine lines of the new Cadillacs. The '48 Cadillac also featured built-in bumpers, powered convertible top, windows and seat, hydramatic transmission and a gas cap hidden behind the taillight. All Cadillacs, except the huge Series Seventy Five models, were new for 1948 (Owner: Jim Gillen)

Above

The slick rounded lines, capped with chrome trim, which would become a Cadillac tradition for years to come flowered on the '48 and '49 models. While the front had been packaged into a one piece look the rear fenders carried on with the older balloon styling

Left

The '48 model was a styling revolution. It brought the front fender line within the bodywork and stamped a new look on modern automobiles. This perfect '48 Series Sixty Two four-door sedan is powered by the last flat head Cadillac V8. In 1949 the flat head would be replaced by what is rightfully considered the first generation of the modern GM OHV V8. This engine was designed by John F Gordon but later handed on to Harry F Barr and Edward N Cole who would father the famous small block Chevrolet V8 (Owner: Keith Remmers)

Above left

The most interesting post-war styling feature was another of Harley Earl's ideas. It had developed from the earlier C-body fastback shape into a two-door sedanet style in this '48 Series Sixty Two powered by the older 346 cubic inch flat head (Owner: Vince Gregoire)

Left

Nineteen-forty-nine was the year of the first one millionth Cadillac. It was sold on 25 November 1949 powered by the new OHV V8. The engine of this '49 Series Sixty One Club Coupe is Cadillac's first 331 cubic inch overhead V8, which developed 160 hp gross. The powerplant had other advantages; it weighed 200 lb less than the old flat head and ran much more efficiently because of its higher compression. The Club Coupe's gracious Harley Earl styling has made it one of the most sought after forties Cadillacs

Above

Based on the last generation of older Cadillac designs built before 1945, this beautiful 'Woody' limousine was custom built for MGM movie studios in Los Angeles, California. Based on the chassis and body of a Fleetwood Series Seventy Five seven-passenger imperial chassis it was restored perfectly by its owner John White. This '49 Woody was built as the age of classic custom-built Cadillacs was slowly coming to an end. The factory has seen the need for luxury transportation and they would set the standard with their own new line of limousines in the 1950s (Owner: Ramshead Collection)

Cadillac 1951 to 1955

Fifty years before, automobiles were virtually unheard of but here, in 1951, a new age of inventions had arrived. Detroit's industrial prowess as an auto manufacturer had returned to a position of dominance and buyers were lined up, waiting to drive a piece of the future. Harley Earl's styling team had done the Sixty One, Sixty Two and the Sixty Special in the latter part of the forties, and now these production sedans, convertibles and Club Coupes were in their second and third years with little in the way of major changes. Body side profiles changed to a more unitised look as the rear fenders were absorbed

Above
The early fifties coupes had a chopped looked reminiscent of many customs. Fiesta Ivory paint complements the red leather interior and the optional white-walls even make the tyres look glamorous

Left
The beginning of the fifties saw Cadillacs mutate in significant but small details. While the front end styling remained mostly the same until 1954, rear end styling was brought inside the bodylines leaving a hint of a fender bulge. The most gracious of the early fifties models was the '51 Coupe De Ville. Its generous proportions and round gracious lines instilled a 'dream car look' to millions (Owner: Wray Tibbs)

inside the main body. Grilles and bumpers also changed but the rest continued mostly with the basic Earl style.

The big news for 1953 was the introduction of air conditioning, 12-volt electrics – and the fabulous Eldorado convertible. It was an image car styled by Fleetwood from Earl's ideas for the General Motors Motorama. This stylish convertible sold only 533 units and was highly expensive at the time. Cadillac titled it in their advertising as 'A car apart – even from other Cadillacs'. It featured Cadillac's first wrap-around windshield, Kelsey Hayes wire wheels, a folding convertible top hidden by a moulded metal 'boot' cover, and was only available in four colours. The Eldorado would evolve further, changing shape with the first 'pointed' rather than 'rounded' P-38 tail fins. The 'dropped beltline' styling continued on through these years and by 1955 it could be found on Cadillacs from Eldorado convertibles to Fleetwood limousines.

Above
Cadillac's golden anniversary was in 1952 and to celebrate all models came with gold 'V' insignias. Under the headlights were more gold decorations that were exclusive to '52 models. Also worth noting was a 30 hp increase to 190; unfortunately weight kept increasing steadily with the power

Left
Convertible sales during the forties fluctuated up and down but averaged around 6000 units a year. While sales in 1952 were not overly impressive, a trend was beginning that would see totals top 14,000 by the start of the next decade

In 1953 Cadillac introduced the Eldorado convertible. Styling was done by Fleetwood with many of the ideas coming from Harley Earl. With wire wheels, a disappearing top, a dropped doorline and a wrap-around windshield, the Eldorado was innovative and expensive, costing a cool $7750. Cadillac described it as: 'A car apart — even from other Cadillacs'

Above left
Cadillacs were given a complete restyling in 1954. Body shape was extensively revised and the Eldorado's wrap-around windshield was installed on all series. Power steering became standard and engine output was up to a healthy 230 hp

Left
The '54 Coupe De Ville's 'C' pillar flows down to and across the trunk, making the roof look almost like a removable hard top. The rear fender no longer dipped before the fin, placing them much higher in relation to the trunk

Above
Although a Cadillac wagon has never been in production, some do exist. This is a custom built four-door on a Sixty Two chassis with Fleetwood doors, a commercial chassis cowl, and numerous other items raided from the Cadillac parts bin. While this wagon is fully loaded, air conditioning could not be installed for the lack of a trunk where the unit normally resides (Owner: Kenneth Turner)

Cadillac 1956 to 1960

By 1956 the 'jet age' had arrived at Cadillac and pointed fins appeared on the rear of the '55 Eldorado. At the end of that year, Harley Earl's P-38 tailfins were replaced by a variety of fin styles designed specifically for each Cadillac model. The base model's engine was bored out to 365 cubic inches and now developed a very healthy 285 bhp. Unveiled in 1955, the fabulous Brougham show car inspired the limited-production Eldorado Brougham four-door. At twice the price of the regular top-of-the-line Cadillac, the opulent Eldorado Brougham cost $13,000 and featured everything from power door locks to dual heating systems, memory seat position, air-dome suspension and suicide rear doors; it was the first American automobile with four headlights. The company's advertising hailed the Brougham as 'Without precedent . . . even in Cadillac's brilliant past!' Distinguished by their stainless steel roofs, 704 Eldorado Broughams were hand-built by Fleetwood in 1957-58.

Something strange happened at Cadillac in 1958 – its products began to look like big Chevrolets. From some angles the styling seemed to be based on some weird genetic mutation rather than any design philosophy. The '58 Sixty Special was dripping with chrome and sculptured bodywork. Some collectors avoid the '58 model, but to others it offers more style, more all-out 'chromemanship' and more pizzazz than the '59. As the decade came to an end, the biggest fins of all time adorned every model from the Fleetwood limousine to the convertible; the 'finned '59' would go down in American folklore as the ultimate iron-dinosaur.

In 1960 the 'fin rage' changed course when Cadillac diminished the huge '59 wing into a stylised peak that was much more in balance with the proportions of the car. Interestingly, the 1959-60 Eldorado Brougham continued the hand-built theme of its forebear, but was now assembled on 'the world's longest production line'. The bodies were fabricated by Pininfarina in Italy and then shipped over to Detroit where Fleetwood applied the final touches. With 345 horses under the hood, the Brougham was no slouch and could glide along effortlessly. The age of the luxury 'muscle car' had arrived. Cadillac was ready to cruise.

The new Eldorado hard top for 1956 added the name tag of 'Seville' while the rag top became the Biarritz. The body kept the '55 styling with only trim changes. This green Seville rides on white wall tyres and gold anodised Kelsey-Hayes alloy wheels (Owner: Dave Miguel)

Above
The post-war trend of more space between the grille bars was reversed in 1956 with this much finer grille. The anodising on the wheels continues to the grille and emblems

Right
Dual four-barrel carburettors on the Eldorados combine to produce 305 hp, a full 20 more than on other models. The Eldorado gold trim theme continues into the engine bay and even the valve covers get the Midas touch of gold factory customising

Above

The interior of this '56 Series Sixty Two displays many options including air-conditioning, a radio, and the Autronic eye – an automatic headlight dimmer. The high-low headlight control was another Cadillac-only option at GM

Left

By the mid 1950s Cadillac were building large automobiles as regular production cars. This superb Series Sixty Two sedan had a massive interior with enough head room to hold a party. Cadillac was once again the 'Mark of Excellence' and reigned supreme as the car of 'The American Dream' (Owner: Patricia Pashukewich)

Most kids in high school like 'hot rods'.
Rob Marian's high school hot rod was
a '57 Fleetwood Limo which he has
now driven for over 30 years. With
300 hp up front, this custom Fleetwood
has been a perennial cruiser
(Owner: Rob Marian)

Above
The new 'shark fin' and revised bumper-exhaust for 1957 are seen in this rear shot of a Sixty Special

Right
All model lines were restyled in 1957 and engine output was once again bumped up, this time to 300 hp. The Sixty Specials had their lower rear quarter panels clad in bright-work, as did this Black Fleetwood, which also features a factory-fitted gold anodised grille (Owner: John McCue)

Above

An unusual feature of this '56 Series Sixty Two is the two-arm brake pedal

Right

In 1957 Cadillac created the ultimate luxury car with the Eldorado Brougham. As planned, the Brougham failed to make money, but the prestige gained was enough to break Packard, the last true competitor of Cadillac. The custom styling included a brushed stainless steel roof and the first production use of quad-headlights on an American car (Owner: Don Weber)

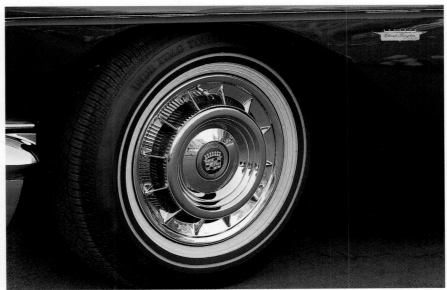

Above
Custom Kelsey-Hayes wheel covers were created for the 700 Broughams and came with the first low profile tyres. These tyres feature both a white wall and yellow wall ring. All part of the differentiation process for this brave and ultimately effective marketing exercise

Left
Nothing was spared in the design and creation of the Brougham's interior. The finest leather was used for the seats while all options for lesser models were standard. Cadillac had thought of everything necessary and unnecessary – there was even a vanity set and perfume dispenser

In keeping with the rest of the car, Cadillac spared little in the creation of the engine. An extra 25 hp was produced for the Brougham with the use of dual four barrels on top of the 365 cubic inch V8. In 1958 power was increased to 335 hp by using three, two barrel carburettors

Above left

The Eldorado Biarritz and Sevilles had model-exclusive styling for 1958. Differences included more chrome and unique front and rear styling. The ten vertical stripes just before the wheel opening are exclusive to the Eldorado and noteworthy (Owner: L D Medley)

Left

All models adopted the Brougham's quad-head lights and received a mild facelift in 1958. Note new lower bumper guards and wider grille on this Seville

Above

With moulded chrome and shark fins sprouting from the trunk, the '58 Eldorado is truly impressive. Note fuel filler below fin

Above
Big changes were in store for Cadillac in 1959. Fins grew to outrageous heights with a complete restyling. Displacement grew to 390 cubic inches and power rose to 325 hp for most models, while the Eldorado boasted 345 hp. Note the Eldorado name on the bottom of the front fender (Owner: Diane Morrow)

Above right
A new double grille was installed in front while a 'dummy' grille was in the rear above the bumper (Owner: Don Turkletop)

Right
Whether gaudy or impressive, the '59 tailfins are enormous. Twin 'bullets' on each fin are used as either tail lights or aircraft navigation beacons! To quote an old adage,, nothing succeeds like excess

Cadillac 1961 to 1965

The beginning of the sixties brought with it a vital new image for Cadillac. Bill Mitchell took up the reins of Harley Earl. Mitchell came from a new school of thought that worked in straight defined lines. This change of direction had come about very pointedly in 1961 with the new 'double fin' rear end treatment. The proportions were new and stylish but the look remained distinctly Cadillac. Bill Mitchell referred to this as the 'chiselled' look. He designed Cadillacs which were slightly smaller and lighter. He did not enjoy the highly decorated look that had been so opulent on the '58 models. There was now far less trim with a resulting $1000 decrease in the base price.

The Eldorado became a convertible-only model while the Sedan De Ville came with a stylish formal roof which gave the back seats enormous head room. Surprisingly the four-door had a more gracious appearance than the two-door Coupe De Ville but both showed a fine line in their design and detailing. Here's how the press described the new generation: 'Silky-smooth, utterly obedient power and luxury have become as much a Cadillac trademark as the name itself'.

Cadillac was making hay even though the American economy experienced a mild downturn in 1961. During this time some ingenious ideas were carried out, among them 'the mink test' which used models wearing mink coats to test the upholstery's compatibility with the garment's fibres. The huge success of the marque led Cadillac to claim that it would take three years to build every variation of model and options without repeating a car.

The '62 models continued with the wrap-around front glass. The rear fender changed shape and the fins faded further into the bodywork, but in 1963 the windshield took on a new profile with a steeper rake and new 'A' pillars. Comfort Control automatic air conditioning and heating temperature systems became optional in 1964. The first totally new engine since 1949 was also introduced; it was a 429 cubic inch V8 which delivered its power via an equally new Turbo Hydra-matic transmission – another Cadillac first.

Bill Mitchell's influence had an enormous impact on Cadillac design; with the '64 and '65 models his chiselled look became 'set in steel' as one of the cleanest shapes ever to grace such a large automobile. For the 1965 model year Cadillac introduced its first telescopic steering column, which could also be tilted as required.

The completely restyled models for 1961 resembled the '59 and '60 Eldorado Broughams. The body shapes were much squarer and fins were reduced in size, although additional fins were added at the bottom of the rear fenders (Owner: Dave Ritchie)

The Cadillac range had grown bigger and so had the cars. All Cadillac models had a sonically balanced exhaust system which lowered noise intrusion. The chassis and body were also specially tuned so they would vibrate at different frequencies and thereby minimise any amplification. The year ended with the slogan: 'There's a new celebrity in town! So new! So right! So obviously Cadillac!'

Above
In the sixties Cadillac continued to reign supreme as 'the car of The American Dream!' For 1962, the split grille returned, a heater/defroster became standard and cornering lights were added. The Coupe De Ville has become a favourite collector's car with its 'quad-fins', which pair off the top fender and bottom fender fins (Owner: David Moon)

Right
Fins were not what they used to be in 1962, but looked as dangerous as ever

Above
Facelifted in 1963, Cadillacs lost their lower fins, making them slab-sided. The once towering fins continued to shrink, as the sixties began to swing

Left
After 1960, Eldorados were offered only as convertibles. By this time the Eldorado had lost much of its uniqueness and relied only on trim to distinguish it from other models (Owner: John White)

Above

The '64 Cadillac followed through on the '63 with only a few cosmetic changes. This was the last year of 'true fins'. For this final year the fins remained the same size but the rear bumper corners took on a kick-out in the centre. This perfect 429-powered Beacon Blue convertible displays the Cadillac 'square-edge' style that endured for many years. This was also the first year for the new Turbo Hydra-matic transmission (Owner: Ed Pashukewich)

Left

Complete with leather bucket seats, the interior of this '64 convertible interior exudes space, comfort and luxury – Cadillac personified

The owner of this '66 Fleetwood Brougham relates owning it to having 'a Pullman railway carriage of your own. It gives you a serene ride with space for a family and a half'. The huge 133 inch wheelbase gives the Brougham almost limousine proportions while the interior provides twin walnut trimmed tables, foot rest, power everything, and matching walnut door caps. Finished in Marlin Blue iridescent, this Brougham is powered by a gas-thirsty 429 cubic inch V8 (Owner: Wray Tibbs)

Left
Vertical headlights were short-lived: twin-headlights came back into fashion after the next model change

Cadillac 1966 to 1970

As in 1960-65, the second half of the sixties would see more innovation and some interesting ideas and products. By 1966 total Cadillac production had exceeded three million. Cadillacs were still considered the ultimate American luxury car. They were long, heavy, powerful and stylish. Except for Lincoln and Chrysler, no other American company built cars of such size or opulence. Cadillac, the 'Standard of the World' still had meaning. In the 'skunk works' at Warren, Michigan, Cadillac had perfected Variable Ratio Power Steering and the company offered it on the '66 model — a first on any US-built car.

In 1966 the Brougham became its own model, selling in the Sixty Special line up as the Fleetwood Brougham four-door. Designed by Fleetwood, this colossal car came with walnut interior trim and sat on a huge 133 inch chassis.

In 1967 Cadillac sold a record 200,000 units. Printed circuits made their debut and Automatic Level Control became standard on some models. But the big news was that engineers had been working on a completely new generation of Eldorado coupes with front-wheel drive. The project began in 1961 as the XP 727 and for a while it was planned with V12 power in mind, but when the

new Eldorado finally reached production in 1967 it was fitted with a V8. The powertrain was developed not at Cadillac, but by GM's Central Research group, and employed the chain-drive, three-speed 'split' automatic transaxle from the Oldsmobile Toronado. It proved to be an excellent marriage. Styled by Bill Mitchell and powered by the trusty 429 cubic inch V8, the '67 Eldorado coupe combined style and comfort with a superb ride and powerful acceleration. The '67 Eldorado is assured of its place in history as the first Cadillac with front-wheel drive, establishing a trend which continues up to the present day. The Eldorado's sharp fenders with 'fade away' hip mouldings as well as its large wheel openings gave a new look to the Cadillac line.

The Eldorado grew significantly in weight and power over the next few model years. In 1970 the Eldorado was offered with a monstrous 500 cubic inch V8. Company advertising proclaimed: 'The Cadillac Eldorado, the only car that can make a Cadillac owner look twice'. The end of the sixties was to be the end of an era. The giant road cars that Cadillac had built so well were to soon lose favour with the emerging oil crisis. Never again would automobiles be built that offered the head and leg room of a small bedroom on wheels. 'Green' politics was upon the automobile and no-one yet liked or understood its implications. The Great Second Age of the American automobile was about to slam shut. The world had an energy crisis on its hands and Detroit had discovered a new word: 'down-sizing'.

Above
The first really new Cadillac since 1957 arrived with the Bill Mitchell-styled '67-68 Fleetwood Eldorado Coupe. Its unique body styling and FWD powertrain gave a new meaning to the Eldorado. Power for this '68 model was supplied by the new 472 cubic inch engine which delivered 375 hp. A V12 engine was designed and tested for the new Eldorado, but the V8 was adopted instead as a cost cutting move (Owner: Bob Hoffmann)

Right
The advertising copy said, 'The World's finest personal car'. Stylist Bill Mitchell had detailed the new Eldorado like a piece of expensive jewellery with clear fine lines and sharp angular corners

Above
Bill Mitchell's fine design work can be seen in this close-up view. The egg-crate grille, hide-away headlights and chiselled body-lines gave the new generation Eldorado a sophisticated style (Owner: John McCue)

Above right
Stacked headlight designs were coming to a close with this '68 De Ville convertible. Fitted with a 10.5 to 1 compression ratio, 375 hp, 472 cubic inch V8, the car had a powerful edge on the competition and rapid acceleration despite its weight. Finished in Kasmir Ivory, the car is fitted with all available power options, Climate Control and Guide-Matic head lamp dimmer (Owner: Ed Pashukewich)

Right
Once again Cadillac's fine attention to detail gave the '68 De Ville convertible a clean, neat appearance with well-proportioned bodywork

Above

Like the '66 Fleetwood Brougham, the '70 De Ville convertible was 'a giant among cars' and presented a spectacular sight of power and luxury that does not come from Detroit today. Powered by the generic Cadillac 472 V8, its 375 hp took good care of the performance needs of its owner. Finished in Chalice Gold this convertible is fully loaded with all power options (seats, top, windows) and front disc brakes

Left

The new for '67 FWD Eldorado body was refreshed and improved for '69; it lost some of its fine-lined elegance with more rotund body moulding and a heavier look to the front end. However, it was still powered by the 472 cubic inch V8 of the '68 Eldorado (Owner: James Maybee)

Cadillac 1971 to 1975

Cadillac began the seventies on a strong note. However, as history would show, nothing is predictable about geopolitics and enrgy resources. In retrospect it was a last hurrah for the formula of bulk power and cubic inches. Stiffer emission laws and the gas crunch would soon take their toll in terms of horsepower, but cubic inches (and therefore bodies) remained large and it would take many years to introduce smaller, more fuel-efficient powerplants. Despite a lengthy strike, some of the new '71 Eldorados were delivered with high compression engines before Cadillac succumbed to the emission legislation later in the year.

Although reported power did not drop between 1971-72, the somewhat optimistic engine ratings only made the switch from gross horsepower 365, to net horsepower 235, seem all the worse. More bad news was to come in the wake of 1973 Middle East conflict. Like every other automobile manufacturer, Cadillac was totally unprepared for the 1974 energy crisis that was triggered by the massive increase in crude oil prices demanded by the Arab-dominated OPEC. Already restrained by environmental protection measures, the desperate need to maximise fuel economy meant that the big 500 cubic inch V8 could only deliver a paltry 190 bhp in 1975.

With so much luxury offered, buyers did not mind the somewhat anaemic engines. Cadillac still had much to offer across the range; increased crash protection, attractive trim options and extensive comfort and in-car entertainment (ICE) options helped to boost sales. There was even a Cadillac (Eldorado) convertible.

Overall, production increased every year until 1973, when it peaked at a record 307,698 – a figure not seen again until 1977. The five millionth Cadillac was built on 27 June, 1973. As if to make 1973 look even better, a Cadillac Eldorado convertible became the Indy 500 pace car. Despite its 500 cubic inches, experts said that the V8 must have been warmed over to enable the car to reach the speeds required. Althoughsales took a sharp drop in 1974, production increased again by 40,000 cars the following year.

In keeping with its tradition of being at the forefront of new technology, Cadillac achieved more firsts in the seventies. A transistorised rear braking

The Eldorado had grown to an enormous size by the early 1970s. Powered by the new 500 cubic inch engine, this factory painted Mountain Laurel is one of four convertibles painted in this colour in 1975. The 'elephant' powerplant was rated at only 190 hp (down from 365 in 1971) due to the new air pollution equipment Cadillac was required to fit (Owner: Laura Lee Evans)

control unit was offered on all cars from 1972. An air cushion restraint system followed in 1974. Electronic fuel injection was also introduced. While no one would call the first half of the seventies a heyday for Cadillac, the range had sold well by offering exactly what the majority of customers wanted. Engine output may have withered, and Cadillac had not yet escaped from all of its woes, but the first steps to a brighter future were already behind them.

Big, slab-sided, body panels graced the '75 Eldorado convertible, which retained the front-wheel drive arrangement that had first appeared on the '67 model. Cadillac still uses an advanced form of this FWD system today

Cadillac 1976 to 1980

The second half of the seventies looked much like an inverse of the first half of the decade. By 1976 Cadillacs had become so big and heavy that a major rethink was required. The new 'down-sized' Seville, introduced in 1975, was a portent of how Cadillacs would look in the years ahead. Although smaller, the Seville offered much in the way of luxury, performance and, because of its size, even fuel economy. Parts of the Seville were of high quality, such as the front and rear disc-brakes introduced in 1977. Other facets were quite cheap; the Seville was offered with only a vinyl top until 1977 to hide the roughly matched roof sections of the Chevrolet Nova with which it shared platforms. Reflecting the demands for greater economy, the '78 Seville was offered with a diesel engine and trip computer. The elegant Seville was, like the first FWD Eldorado in 1967, a landmark car for Cadillac.

The mid and late seventies required serious cars for a serious time. This philosophy left no room for convertibles, which were disappearing at a tremendous rate. The Eldorado soft top outlasted all but the Jeep, but it was killed off in 1976. Buyers flocked to own 'the last convertible' – and promptly destroyed any chance of the car becoming a rare limited edition. Cadillac advertising hyped the '76 Eldorado convertible with: 'Today a classic, tomorrow a collectors' item'. And 'The '76 Eldorado Convertible . . . last of a magnificent breed'. In many ways they were right and wrong. It was not the last convertible, but it was the 'last of a magnificent breed'.

The Eldorado hard-top continued unchanged until 1979 when it received a complete redesign. Suitably down-sized, the new car had a shortened wheelbase and weight was reduced by a full 1200 pounds, helping to improve economy to a respectable 20 mpg. The Eldorado's styling was also changed drastically, with a much more contemporary and handsome body.

Cadillac said good-bye to the big convertible in 1976. The last 200 were white on white and had a special plaque on the dashboard. Cadillac kept the final example off the production line and fitted it with a license plate that read 'LAST'. However, the company later had a change of heart and began producing convertibles again in 1983 (Owner: David France)

Above
The Coupe De Ville was one of Cadillac's most popular models, and offered its
fortunate owners plenty of luxury and style. It came with a padded vinyl top and wire
wheel covers; customers could specify metallic paint. Power came from a new 425
cubic inch V8 with optional fuel injection (Owner: Elaine Ilderton)

Above right
The four-door version of the Coupe De Ville was called the Sedan De Ville. It featured
a different roof line, but all sheet metal up front was interchangeable between the
coupe and the sedan

Right
Cadillacs and limousines go hand in hand. The vast majority of American rented limos
were (and still are) Cadillacs. While there are many aftermarket converted limos, most
are the factory built Cadillac Series Seventy Fives. The '76 Series Seventy Five
measured a full 252.2 inches in length and was propelled by a 500 cubic inch V8
(Owner: Gerald R Steinard)

Above

Despite being the smallest Cadillac, the Seville offered superb luxury with economy. A sign of the times was that customers for the '78 Seville could have a trip computer and, remarkably for a Cadillac, an optional diesel engine

Left

Targeted at the Mercedes-Benz 450, the '77 Seville had disc brakes all-round and was equipped with a fuel injected 350 cubic inch engine that produced almost as much power as the outdated 500 and 425 units (Owner: Patricia Pashukewich)

Opposite
In 1980 Cadillac introduced the new Seville with front-wheel drive and radical new styling. A 105 hp diesel engine was standard, offering unprecedented economy but truly sluggish acceleration. Conventional petrol-engined models delivered performance more in keeping with the Seville's exceptional ride and competent handling

Above
While the appearance of the front end did not change much on the Seville (except for the grille), the 'bustle back' styling made the new front-wheel drive models very easy to distinguish from earlier machines

Cadillac 1981 to 1985

By the early eighties Cadillac had an established range of front-wheel drive, 'down-sized' cars. The experience Cadillac had gained with the front-wheel drive Eldorado, and what its GM-partner Chevrolet had learned with their FWD range, was assimilated into the design of a new product range.

The Eldorado had developed into something of a cult car, many owners being repeat customers. In 1982 those lucky enough to have some extra cash to spend could order the Special Edition Eldorado Touring Coupe: 'Created for the person who loves to drive'. It utilised the same mechanicals as the standard Eldorado, but came with special trim, wheels and uprated Touring suspension

Left
Restyled for 1979, the Eldorado lost 1200 lbs in the process of improving fuel economy and acceleration. Despite being the smallest Eldorado in history, the new car offered a standard of luxury equal to earlier Cadillacs and far superior handling, especially with the Touring package (Owners: Ken and Vicky Reeves)

Above
The Cadillac soft-top returned in 1984, much to the dismay of the 1976 'last convertible' buyers. An unsuccessful law suit was brought against the company, though most people were happy to see a sign of good times return (Owner: Marvin Pashukewich)

that improved handling without sacrificing ride quality. The Eldorado was by now riding on a chassis with a 113.9 inch wheelbase. A smaller, more economical 368 cubic inch fuel-injected V8 was now standard, but was inevitably much less powerful (at 145 bhp) than the awesome motors of yesteryear.

In the Seville you could now order a diesel V8. This lump was based on the Chevy 350 cubic inch unit and was rated at a miserable 105 hp. The coming of the FWD Seville also heralded another modern first for Cadillac: all-wheel fully independent suspension. Styled by Wayne Kady while working with the great Bill Mitchell, the Seville's classic English bodywork attracted a new set of buyers looking for something special.

The introduction of the Gold Key Delivery System had earned Cadillac a 'Number One' sales satisfaction rating from the prestigious J D Power and Associates.

Also new in 1982, the Cimarron was sadly little more than a Chevy with Cadillac trim. Based on the GM J-car series, its 85 hp four-cylinder engine was a post-war first for Cadillac. The Cimarron was not a bad car, particularly with V6 power, and it sold in quite large numbers. But it lacked the quality and refinement of a true Cadillac and was eventually dropped from the line-up in mid 1984.

Above
While not noticeable from the side, small fins are present on this Biarritz convertible

Left
Interiors of the early eighties Eldorados were modern and comfortable, although the digital instruments on the dashboard did not meet with universal approval...

Cadillac 1986 to 1990

Cadillac heralded the 1986 De Ville with the ad line 'Best of all . . . It's a Cadillac'. The age of the huge, gas-guzzling Cadillac had ended and new leaner, lighter products were being introduced. New air pollution regulations and the 1974 oil crisis had forced the company to drastically reduce the power of its engines, but by the end of the decade 'power and luxury' were again dominant Cadillac themes.

Early attempts to combine reasonable economy and performance were not encouraging. Designed for the new generation of smaller, front-wheel drive Cadillacs, the all-aluminium 4.1 litre V8 that came on stream at the beginning of the decade delivered a mere 130 hp. A much improved 4.5 litre version was introduced in 1988, initially rated at 155 hp but subsequently developed to produce 180 hp for 1990.

Launched in 1987, the Allante was the first production two-seater Cadillac roadster of modern times (the earlier Le Mans and Cyclone were concept cars). Another first for the car was its use of multi-plexed wiring to control external lighting. Designed and built by Pininfarina of Italy, the Allante was originally fitted with the then new 4.5 litre V8 rated at 170 hp.

A series of significant safety improvements began with the '86 De Villes and Fleetwoods, which both received ABS braking systems, while the '89 Allante came with traction control; air bags were introduced across the range in 1990. Safety of different kind arrived when Cadillac implemented a 24-hour emergency roadside service to help stranded owners continue on their way after a highway breakdown. A Cadillac's progress is rarely interrupted by mechanical failure, but this caring approach to customer relations has helped to re-establish the company's reputation for quality and integrity.

The Seville, in common with the Eldorado, had become a somewhat ponderous car to drive; this was cured by introducing independent rear suspension on its 108-inch wheelbase, which not only gave a 'Cadillac ride' but also improved the vehicle's overall handling and stability.

Even as the 75th Anniversary of the Cadillac V8 was being celebrated in 1989, the traditional square-edged, gold trimmed designs were giving way to new aerodynamic shapes created for the 1990s ...

The Seville was restyled in 1986, losing the previous generation's bustle-back. It retained the 4.1 litre all-aluminium V8 and had fully independent suspension. A trunk mounted spare tyre was one of a number of dealer options on this model

Cadillac 1991 to 1993

General Motors had been getting a bad lashing from the media about building cars that weren't up to scratch with the imports. Much of the press claimed that the GM Divisions had lost touch with what the customer wanted in terms of style, quality or performance. But none of the doom-sayers had seen much of what Cadillac was about to do. The 1990s would herald a new generation of Cadillac products that were better built, styled superbly, and offered all the luxury, comfort and performance that buyers could want.

Two new models led off in 1992, the Seville and the Eldorado. Both cars would both prove to be instant hits and sell out before the model year ended. Competition from high quality Japanese imports had fragmented the US market for luxury automobiles, but Cadillac responded with a new line of gracious, well-proportioned vehicles that offered the younger, more sports oriented buyer an 'American-Made' alternative. Suddenly, the typical Cadillac customer was under 50 years old. 'Why America is more Comfortable with Cadillac' was more than just advertising hype. By the beginning of the 1990s, Cadillac could stand alone and offer a car that could run with the pack, would handle and stop with impressive ease, while providing the style that once made Cadillac such a hallowed name. The De Ville was thoroughly revised with a Touring Sedan Package that offered enhanced acceleration and a firmer suspension set up as well as standard Computer Command Ride.

The Brougham continues as Cadillac's last full-sized, rear-wheel drive model and also retains its claim as 'The longest production automobile'. Available with either a 5.0 litre or a 5.7 litre fuel injected V8, the Brougham is not subject to a gas-guzzler tax.

Finally in 1993 the long awaited Northstar 32-valve V8 arrived. Fitted to the Allante and the Seville STS, this 300 hp engine delivers smooth and powerful acceleration with great gas mileage. Cadillac, 'The Standard of the World' in an earlier automobile age, has not rested on its laurels, having reclaimed its title as the builder of some of the world's finest luxury automobiles.

The latest generation of Sevilles has served notice on other luxury car builders that Cadillac is back and ready to play games at virtually any speed. The stunning new Seville STS (Sport Touring Sedan) sold out in 1992 with the 200 hp 4.9 litre V8. The STS then upped the stakes with modified suspension and the stunningly smooth 300 hp 32-valve Northstar V8. Not surprisingly, performance is exceptionally lively and handling is first class. Interior space, smoothness and style are blended together in the Seville, a car for the person who wants the ultimate in power, performance and luxury

Above

The star of the show is the slick Cadillac Allante sports roadster, which is also available with an optional hardtop. Now propelled by the 4.6 litre Northstar 32-valve V8, which slams 300 hp to the road through a four-speed transmission using Traction Control, the Allante is indeed a hot rocket. The Allante body and interior are built in Italy by Pininfarina and flown across the Atlantic by Boeing 747F freighter to Detroit, where the powertrain is installed and each vehicle is tested on a special Allante test track before delivery. The car comes with Road Sensing Suspension, air bag, Traction Control and ABS

Left

The Sedan De Ville has been a long term favourite with Cadillac buyers. This new generation FWD sedan offers great interior space, power, handling and style for up to six passengers. The Speed Sensitive suspension and matching power steering systems adds to the power of the newly refined 4.9 litre V8 and its matching electronic four-speed automatic transmission. The Sedan De Ville can sprint from 0 to 60 mph in 9.1 seconds

Above
Brougham styling, while continuing as the least modern in the Cadillac line, is also the most formal

Left
Cadillac continues to set the standard for limousines. Numerous conversions, as well as factory built limos, are created on the Brougham chassis

Above left

The Brougham is the last hold-out of big rear-wheel drive sedans at Cadillac. Powered by a 5.0 litre V8 rated at 105 hp, it could be optioned up with a 5.7 litre V8 delivering 175 hp. The Brougham's traditional frame and body construction have kept it a favourite with limousine builders and companies that specialise in car conversions. As old as this technology may be, the Brougham does come with anti-lock brakes and fuel injection

Left

The Cadillac De Ville series was, at the beginning of the 1990s, America's best selling luxury automobile. Sold in both sedan and coupe form, it came with a FWD 4.5 litre V8. This new version of the old 4.1 litre all-aluminium V8 snapped the horsepower rating up to 180 and gave the Coupe De Ville a rapid rise in its performance potential. This new generation of cars represented a turning point in quality and sales, combining all the best features, options and looks into a product line which stamped a new meaning on Cadillac style

Above

The Seville STS was another great Cadillac from the early nineties. It took its style from the older Eldorado Touring Coupe and blended those ideas with a new interior and drive ratio. The result was a sports sedan with four bucket seats, full length console, a performance suspension package and new 16 inch alloy wheels; 0 to 60 mph took less than nine seconds

Above

The '91 Eldorado Touring Coupe was powered by the 4.5 litre V8 that produced 200 hp and 275 lb/ft of torque. In its optioned form as a Touring Coupe, the Eldorado could cut a dash on Main Street while eating up the twisties on back country two-lanes. Its anti-lock brakes and reworked touring suspension system rolled on 16 inch alloy wheels, while inside every power option from windows and doors to seats and cruise control came with a seating package that could take you a thousand miles a day in perfect comfort

Above right

The Cadillac Fleetwood Sixty Special may look like a rear-wheel drive car, but it too used the FWD 4.9 litre V8 that put out 200 horses. The Sixty Special was a limited production 'executive class' sedan with six-passenger seating and featured real American Walnut with leather seats styled by Italian designer Giugiaro of Ital Design. The Fleetwood Sixty was fully loaded with all accessories and exemplified the high style that Cadillac set for its own class of luxury

Right

The Sedan de Ville continued to be Cadillac's top seller. It was popular for a number of reasons: it was extremely price competitive in terms of luxury, performance, ride and style, while its powertrain provided ample performance from the 4.9 litre V8; Computer Command Ride suspension improved high-speed stability and handling

Above

This artist concept of how the new '93 Brougham will look as an extended wheelbase limousine is fascinating. Even with its increased wheelbase, this limousine looks like a regal automobile. The rounded lines and chrome trim enhance its style without going over the top

Left

The '93 Eldorado Sport Coupe is the elite performance model of the Eldorado range. Fitted with the 295 hp Northstar V8, the Sports Coupe offers all the 'bells and whistles' – Traction Control, four-channel ABS brakes and Road Sensing performance suspension. The 32-valve four-cam Northstar engine can sprint the coupe from 0 to 60 mph in a road-burning 7.5 seconds. On the luxury side the Sport Coupe also leaves very little to wish for with a massive list of standard power and comfort features which both dazzle the mind and cosset the body

Above

The '93 Cadillac Brougham is the ultimate 'big' Cadillac; in its stock form it can accommodate six people with ease but is designed so both Cadillac and the aftermarket have a perfect product for building extended wheelbase ('stretched') limousines. Powered by a standard 5.7 litre V8 the Brougham is the only rear-wheel drive Cadillac in 1993. The Brougham also features all new bodywork, twin air bags, traction control and ABS. Options include a Coachbuilder package, Armoring Package and an Export package

Right

The Allante was chosen to be the Indy 500 Pace Car for 1992. This job required the Allante to be capable of leading the race cars on the warm-up lap or to be able to take the lead at any time should it be necessary to slow the race into a holding pattern while accidents are cleared. It was the first showing of the powerful new 32-valve Northstar V8. This produced a 0 to 60 mph time of under seven seconds and top speed of 150 mph. For the event Cadillac built three special 290 hp versions complete with roll bars, strobe lights and on-board fire safety equipment. Another 83 Allantes were fitted out with special 'Pace Car' graphics for parades, as official cars and for display purposes

The '93 STS Seville powered by the 295 hp Northstar V8 is a bold and fast car to drive. Its race handling and sensational turn of speed make it one the America's finest sports sedans to date, with a top speed of 150 mph and a 0 to 60 mph time of 7.5 seconds. The STS's superb styling and class-competitive performance offers a American alternative to the European sports sedans that have dominated the market for many years

The '91 Brougham has been a favourite among the coachbuilding community. This hearse shows how graciously the Brougham can be re-bodied into a custom built conversion

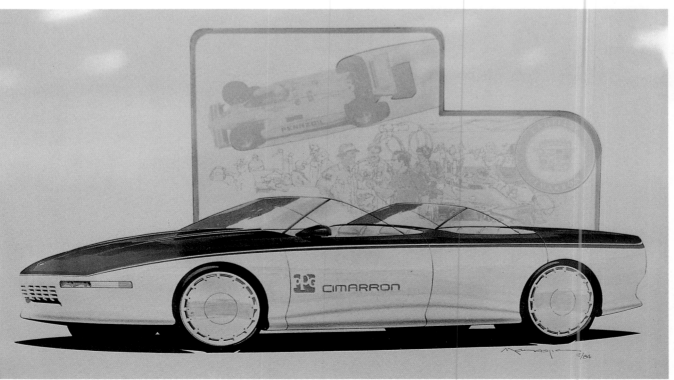

CADILLAC-TODAY AND THE FUTURE

The American-built luxury automobile market suffered heavily during the 1980s; European manufacturers of high performance and luxury automobiles took full advantage of the fact that Detroit was not building the type of cars that well-heeled customers wanted to own. With a pressing need for change, Cadillac brought some hot new talent into the design studios. Despite its solid base of regular customers, Cadillac knew that without a new and truly competitive product range it would wither and die on the vine as European and Japanese manufacturers continued to exploit the 'quality gap'.

During the eighties a series of inspirational concept cars, most notably the Voyage, Solitar and Aurora showed the way ahead. These imaginative vehicles were never intended to go into production, but they enabled designers and engineers to experiment with new shapes and create the ideal blend of luxury, performance and style. Designers like Dennis Little, Ben Salvador, Larry Erickson, Dick Dunn and Scott Wassell worked closely with a talented team of engineers; everyone was fired up to get the job done and put Cadillac back on top. This process was not to be a 'wash-job'!

Dennis Little is currently the chief exterior designer at Cadillac's Advance Design Studio in Warren, Michigan and as such is the man responsible for how Cadillacs will look in the 1990s. When the new vision of what Cadillac could be was brought to light, the teams were given a free hand to decide what direction they would move in to make Cadillac a revered name again. According to Dennis Little they decided to 'Design a car that they would want to own, one with a true luxury look and quality that would deliver the kind of performance you would expect from a high performance sports sedan'. Cadillac dealt with the basics first and then worked and reworked every idea. The exercise involved more than just designing pretty cars. Enter the Northstar, a new 32-valve, four cam 270 bhp engine and one of the most superbly engineered V8s seen for many years. (It reached the production lines in 1993.) Cadillac's major change in thinking and design was revealed in 1992 with the launch of the stunning new Seville, STS and Eldorado. All three cars sold out before the end of the model year.

Left
Dennis Little is the man responsible for Cadillac's 'New Look'. Dennis is head of exterior design at Cadillac's Advanced Design Studios in the GM Tech Center in Warren, Michigan. His conceptual work goes from original drawing to final style. Dennis does not work alone. He has a team of the hottest young design talent in the country to get the job done just right

The future now looks bright at Cadillac; a new found confidence is noticeable and team spirit is riding high. Workers and managers believe they are building world class products and are determined to back them up with a level of assembly and service that is second to none. And they have the tools to finish the job. The Detroit/Hamtramck assembly plant is one of the most advanced automobile manufacturing facilities in North America. The Seville and Allante are both assembled at this facility under the most rigorous procedures. The plant builds Sevilles from stamped galvanised steel panels, rust-protects them by fully immersing the body shell in a paint bath, and then paints on the final colour with robots before the cars are finally assembled – all under one roof. The combination of design and production have come together in the

Above

In the design process full-scale lofting and illustrations are done to make sure all dimensions are correct and to help the model makers get their shapes and forms exactly right. Here a designer adds detail with an air-brush to a final full-colour illustration of the Aurora concept car

Left

The Aurora concept car is Cadillac's idea of a new international Cadillac. The Aurora is powered by the existing 4.5 litre SPFI V8 driving all four wheels. Not only is the Aurora AWD, but traction control is present at each wheel. Cadillac decided that in today's market a luxury car must appeal to an international buyer. With this in mind they designed the Aurora to look as good on the autobahn as it does on the interstate

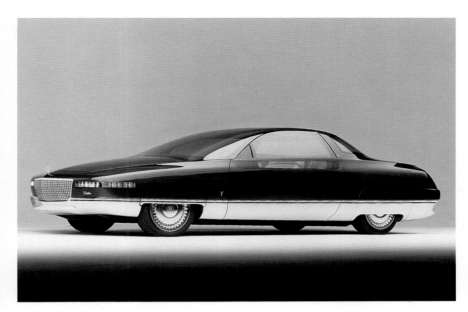

1990s with a firm re-stamp of the 'Cadillac-look'. The combination of luxury and performance in the automobiles that Cadillac is building today, and the products it is designing for the future, are surely re-establishing and reinforcing the marque's pre-eminence among the luxurycar makers of the world: and that position has been reached without sacrificing that unique Cadillac feel in the name of short-term expediency.

Above

The Solitaire's radical styling and advanced design offered a taste of the future with V12 power from GM design staff. This, the ultimate aerodynamic Eldorado of tomorrow, is a four-place, two-door coupe featuring 'gun-slit' windows in the lower door panels, four fender skirts and a moulded glass greenhouse. The interior features temperature controlled glass tinting, video rear vision system and powered seat with massage controls

Left

Power for the Solitaire had to be on par with the radical styling and advanced design of the car. With this in mind Cadillac entered a joint venture with Lotus to produce a V12 engine. With four camshafts, 48 valves and a capacity of 6.6 litres, the engine produces 430 hp and 480 lb/ft of torque

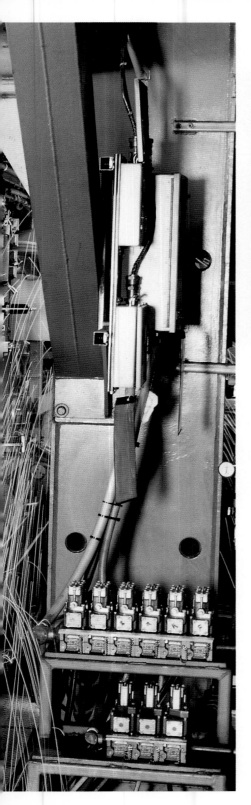

Above

The almost finished product roles down the Hamtramck assembly line. Painted by robots, the Cadillac's production quality standards are some of the most rigorous in the world

Left

At Cadillac's Detroit-Hamtramck assembly plant, Sevilles and Eldorados are assembled using robotic welders. Made of pre-galvanized steel except for the roof, the body shells move from pressed metal to final assembly in only a few hours

The Voyage is a four-door concept sedan for the 21st century. John O Grettenberger, Cadillac's general manager, referred to the Voyage as 'a rolling laboratory', pointing out its leading-edge traction technology. Under normal driving the rear wheels transmit power but traction sensors switch to all-wheel drive if needed. Power is supplied from a production Cadillac 4.5 litre aluminium V8 modified to produce a snappy 270 hp

Rad Cad

Customising automobiles has been an American tradition since the 1930s and Cadillacs have not escaped this surgery and remaking. Custom Cadillacs are certainly nothing new, having existed since the early days of motoring. Not only were they built in America, there were coach builders in Switzerland, Italy, England and France who tackled the American iron. The popularity of hot rodding and custom cars burgeoned in the 1980s and folks who dreamed of 'greater things automotive' have produced some spectacular results. Billy F Gibbons from the Texan rock and roll band 'ZZ Top' had Larry Erickson design him the wildest custom Cadillac in history when he penned out the now famous CADZZILLA™. Others like Jay Orhberg have allowed their imagination to run riot with wild wheels like the 'Elvis Guitar Cadillac' and the 'World's Longest Limo'. The little guy is not forgotten, either. 'Cow-de-lac', a tongue-in-cheek fun car, has cow skin paint work on a chop-topped weekend fun cruiser. Cadillacs have come to take a place in the hearts of many folks and, for them, just driving 'a Cad' is not enough. Sometimes you have to just do what your heart tells you, even if it is weird, wild or just plain wonderful.

This 'Cow-de-lac' is a student cruiser from Sacramento, California. Complete with mottled cow markings, horns, and a wagging tail powered by a windscreen wiper motor sticking through the trunk, this one-time Coupe De Ville runs a turbocharger on its 429 cubic inch engine

Above
Limousine length has become a status symbol in America. Jay Ohrberg from Burbank, California decided to build the world's largest limo of 64 feet. He commissioned Dick Dean to do the chopping and stretching. However, he was later shamed into lengthening this one to 104 feet, to retain his title as builder of the 'World's Longest Limo'

Right
Unknown to many, Cadillac offered a special 'Elvis Guitar' package in the seventies that included some minor body modifications and a pink paint job. Window tinting was standard and a 1500 watt amplifier was available – although most were ordered as 'acoustical'. This is the 'Elvis Guitar Cadillac', a tongue-in-cheek show car built by Jay Ohrberg to use as a centre piece at international auto shows

Above
This one-time Coupe De Ville is now a true 'Land Yacht'. The owner converted a number of coupes to 'flying bridge' land yachts as a draw card to advertise shops and businesses. This one was discovered doing sterling service in front of a smog testing station in Los Angeles

Above right
The '76 through '80 Seville was one of the most interesting Cadillacs of modern times. Unlike its bigger brother, the Brougham, which often received the stretched limo treatment, the Seville was shortened or reassembled on the same chassis in some very interesting combinations. This shortened convertible made a weird two-seater

Right
Amazingly this '79 Seville custom sits on a stock wheelbase. The body was cut into sections and re-positioned on the chassis to give the hood the appearance of an older '30s personal coupe with two side-mounted tyres and a setback cabin

Above

Bob and Greg Westbury from Concord, California built this wild custom from a '49 Cadillac Coupe De Ville. Greg is well known for his exquisite hot rods and Bob wanted a perfect custom cruiser. They built this 'peach' between them powered by a 454 big block Chevrolet. The body features all the custom tricks, including a removable roof made from factory steel, moulded bumpers, shaved trim, billet alloy wheels, pro-street chassis and silver paintwork with wild purple scallops

Left

The Shark-Mobile was built by Frank DeRosa from Pittsburg, California. Frank took a 1960 Coupe De Ville, sliced off the roof, chopped and sectioned it and then added in a Buick Riviera backlight and roof moulding. The rest of the body was radically customised with frenched and shaved panels, blue flake metallic paint and flames. The suspension was radically lowered and the interior was customised with four bucket seats

This is the wildest Cad of them all. CADZZILLA™ is the brain child of Billy F Gibbons
from the legendary rock and roll band 'ZZ Top'. From its hand-built body to its
traditional Moon tank in the grille, it screams 'Drive Me'. Billy F Gibbons commissioned
Larry Erickson, a hot young GM Cadillac designer to modernise and 'hot rod' a fabled
'48 Sixty-Two Cadillac Club Coupe sedanet. The work was done at Boyd Coddington's
shop in Los Angeles and included a completely new tube chassis, Corvette front
suspension, mega-inch Cadillac V8 and four-bar rear end. CADZZILLA™ is the
copyright of GIZMOCHINE, INC 1991, all rights reserved